TAKING *the* "*I*" *out of* CLIENTELE

A Retailer's Guide to Selling Better Than You Can Sell

Cheryl Beall

iUniverse, Inc.
New York Lincoln Shanghai

Taking the "I" out of Clientele
A Retailer's Guide to Selling Better Than You Can Sell

iUniverse books may be ordered through booksellers or by contacting:

iUniverse
2021 Pine Lake Road, Suite 100
Lincoln, NE 68512
www.iuniverse.com
1-800-Authors (1-800-288-4677)

ISBN-13: 978-0-595-41369-0 (pbk)
ISBN-13: 978-0-595-85718-0 (ebk)
ISBN-10: 0-595-41369-2 (pbk)
ISBN-10: 0-595-85718-3 (ebk)

Printed in the United States of America

With thanks to my husband Eric, who turned this "I" to "we".

Contents

Introduction

Psst.

What if I told you that I knew a secret—a tip that could not only transform your career as a sales professional, but also maybe even change your life? What if I could flip a switch that would not only help you win over new customers, but also turn strangers into friends? What if I promised not merely to improve your performance on the sales floor, but also to deliver you from moments of social distress: the cocktail party full of unknown faces, the blind date that lives up to its billing. What if I told you that the answer was in fact a question—a question to which you already know the answer?

What if it's not all about you?

Go ahead—exhale. Feel the relief, as a sack of worries is suddenly lifted from your shoulders. Imagine a day without that endless inner monologue:

> *"What will I say what will I sell how do I close and will I earn my spiff?"*

Imagine an evening without the perpetually nagging voice of Miss Party of One:

> *"You don't know a soul here, and the shoes were an unfortunate choice.*
> *Let's hope you have something terribly clever to say…"*

If we could wriggle out from under our relentless self-scrutiny long enough to realize that we are not actually the center of the universe—not even our own—then we would learn what every successful artist, athlete, actor, and public speaker knows from experience: our self-awareness is only a hindrance to our own performance. The more present we are in our own mind, the more we get in our own way. We are at our most creative and engaging when we are so absorbed in our task that we are hardly aware of what we're doing.

The truth is, Taking the "I" Out of Clientele is not just an effective sales strategy. It's a life skill. It can make us confident without being cocky, at ease without being flippant. In business, it can allow us to see opportunities where others see only obstacles, to innovate in ways that directly meet our customers' needs. So often, we're staring in a window but missing what's happening inside because we're too busy checking our own appearance in the reflection. When we can move ourselves from star to supporting actor in the story of our own lives, we can finally focus on what is truly important:

The relationship.

Whether it's a cocktail party or a sales call, a job interview or a customer return, the goal of any social interaction should always be the same: to build a relationship with another person. Of course, the only way to do this is to put aside our self-reflection and begin to see the other person, or people, in front of us. At last, we can realize that everyone is not staring at us—they're too occupied with their own lives. We don't have to "make" conversation. We just need to inquire about the person across from us and be ready to listen with interest. We don't need to impress, or promote, or "sell." We just need to learn who the other person is, discover what they need or want, and try to meet that need.

In any social situation, most of our discomfort results from self-consciousness. We wonder:

"Do I look foolish?"

"Will I achieve my goal?"

"Will I be rejected?"

Most conventional selling techniques offer only tricks to get past the awkwardness of approaching strangers, making conversation, or persuading them into a purchase. But if our focus moves from ourselves to other people, we no longer need to put on an "act." We can simply be ourselves and react to the other person. When we keep our eyes on our clients rather than ourselves, we're not only better sellers; we're better people. We might even make some friends along the way.

Sadly, this doesn't come naturally. It runs against our finely honed instincts of self-interest and desire for approval. So what follows is a step-by-step guide to help us get past our own fabulousness on the selling floor—to remind us of what we need to do to get the "I" out of our selling. We'll learn how to put our focus back where it belongs: on the client.

This is not a passive exercise. Taking the "I" Out of Clientele isn't a reconnaissance mission to study the customer and wait for something to happen. It is an active engagement, with very specific techniques and strategies. Once we've established a relationship, we need to make that relationship work to our benefit and to the benefit of our company—and our clients. We'll begin by discovering how to pull ourselves out of our selling approach, and then we'll find ways to redirect our energy and attention toward the customer and into action.

Perhaps all of this sounds suspiciously like advice your mother gave you long ago: don't be selfish; be mindful of the feelings of others; be helpful to strangers. When I was young, I was painfully shy. To make matters worse, my family moved frequently. Sending me out to start first grade at a new school, my mother offered the following advice:

> *"At recess, just march up to any child you see on the playground, smile, and say: 'Hello, my name is Cheryl. Do you want to be my friend?'"*

Whatever the approach lacked in sophistication, it did succeed in unveiling the secret underlying all social interaction. We only succeed by putting our self-consciousness aside and reaching out to others. The true currency of human existence is not money. It is relationships.

Clerks have customers. Sales people have clients. But genuine sales professionals have something more: friends. That makes for a better life—and better business.

"Don't Snob. Hobnob!"

TAKING the "I" out of CLIENTELE

TAKING *the* "*I*" *out of* CLIENTELE

Strange, isn't it, what a poor reputation the whole idea of "selling" has developed over the past few decades? After all, the "salesman" is essential to the whole idea of business. It's not enough to produce a good or service, or market it, or advertise it. Sooner or later, someone has to approach the customer and bring home the sale. The relationship of buyer and seller is as much a part of the fabric of our society as teacher and student, or parent and child.

And yet, just to say the word "salesman" is to conjure up a whole selling floor full of stereotypes, none of them overly flattering. Let's meet a few of these folks.

In one corner, we find the **Part-Time Clerk**. Even when employed full-time, this sales-floor standby only works part-time, preferring to devote his or her hours to chatting on the phone or commiserating with other sales associates, while the customer fumes at the counter. In another corner, over near the mirrors, we observe the **Statue of Style**. Behold this monument to personal grooming and elevated self-esteem, who assumes the role of living mannequin as he or she waits in vain for the appearance of a customer worthy of attention.

At least providing some signs of life is the booming voice of the **King of Persuasion**, whose fast-talking recitation of "The 600 Best Reasons to Purchase Today" seems to send the customers careening toward the exits instead of the cash-wrap. And of course, who could forget **Jaws the Sales-Floor Shark**. Enter customer, cue ominous music, and watch the predator in action—pouncing quickly, pushing relentlessly, ever closing, with bared teeth on a hapless "swimmer."

BECAUSE THEY ARE FLUENT TALKERS, MANY YOUNG MEN GET THE IDEA THAT THEY ARE *natural born Salesmen*, WHEN WHAT NATURE INTENDED THEM TO BE WAS *Barbers*.

As serious sales professionals, we could deride these characters as fictitious generalizations, fodder for cocktail party horror stories. Except that we've met them. After all, we're not only sellers; we are also buyers. We've watched our own afternoon shopping spree turn from *Pretty Woman* to *Night of the Living Dead*. If we're being honest, we'd have to admit that even on our own selling floor there are probably people that fit quite comfortably into each stereotype.

As different as they are, what all of these salesman types have in common is that none of them have learned to take the "I" out. Everything is all about them—their attention, their vanity, their knowledge, their commission. The customer is an annoyance, an audience, or a victim, but not a client—and never will be. No wonder the buyer/seller relationship is in dire straits. When a customer stands in the store and thinks, "I must be invisible," he or she has no idea how right that is. When a salesperson's "I's" are in the wrong place, the client quite literally disappears.

The truth is, even the best of us can find that our focus needs readjusting. The daily pressures of doing business can blind us with details and trivia. Even our own ambition or desire to please can work against us. Before long, we have become absorbed in our own world and have left the customer standing outside on the street.

What we need is a method to redirect our energies, to counter our own instincts, and in some sense to actually reverse the selling process. Taking the "I" Out of Clientele means standing the traditional selling approach on its head, and then watching the world come into its right focus. So let's start with "The Don'ts and Do's of Selling"—a simple checklist for our bedroom mirror, refrigerator, or work locker, reminding us each day to do less and see more.

Let the Part-Timers have their leisure, and the Statues stand their ground. Let the Kings of Persuasion pontificate, and the Sharks take their bites. As true sales professionals, we can move beyond the stereotypes to something genuine, graceful, and rewarding in every sense of that word.

A musician once said, "It's the notes that you don't play that make the music." Other than the piped-in sound of Muzak, we don't hear much music being made on the selling floor these days. The buyer/seller relationship has become an awkward dance, with the salesperson too often leading when he or she should be following. Our success depends as much on what we don't do, as on what we do. The Don'ts and Do's of Selling remind us that if we let the customer set the tempo and establish the direction, we can both get where we're going together, buyer and seller, in a way that is easy, graceful, and maybe even a little enjoyable.

The DON'Ts and DO's of Selling

DON'T LEAP. _Look_

If we wish to see the primal laws of the jungle in action, we don't need to tune into _Wild Kingdom_. A simple trip to the local mall should do the trick. We can stand outside the store of our choice and watch the forces of nature have their way. See the predators circling inside, lying in wait for their hapless prey. A customer enters and instantly the hunt is on; the hungry sales force swoops in for the attack. No time for hesitation now. The carnivores are in hot pursuit and this race will go to the swiftest. Or will it?

It's only natural to think so. After all, we're sellers, right? Our instinct is to _sell_. And so much of our experience tells us to act fast. He who hesitates is lost, so we'd better strike while the iron is hot. We don't want to miss an opportunity.

Well…move too fast and we will probably do just that: lose. Indeed, those first few moments, before we've actively engaged the customer, offer a golden opportunity—one that's impossible to recover. This is our moment of observation, in which we form our first impression. We gather all of the clues we can from appearance and body language, in order to determine the strategy of our initial approach.

To lose this crucial time in the interaction is to rush in blindfolded. As soon as we engage with the customers, the selling process is underway and our moment of unobstructed viewing is gone. It's a bit like taking a road trip with my husband. There I am trying to read a map as he hurtles along at breakneck speed. Because we're already moving, it's impossible to locate where we are and even more difficult to determine where we're going. So my advice to you is the same I give to him:

> Stop. *Just stop for a second. Take a breath, and take a good look around. Read the signs. Don't leap. Look.*

Now before we go too far, let's be very clear what this means. I'm not suggesting that customers be ignored for five minutes, while we slyly compile an entire dossier of their personal mannerisms, quirks, and fashion *faux pas*. No customer should enter our store without some sort of acknowledgement, whether it's a "hello" or a simple smile.

But after that acknowledgement, we can take a deep breath and, for the next 30 seconds, simply use our eyes to plan the path ahead. Try really watching someone for 30 seconds. It's actually quite a long time. It's certainly more than enough time to read the basic buying signals. It should be sufficient to pick up most of the other essential information that will determine our selling strategy—without us having to say or do anything at all.

Of course, this is the point. Just by taking a 30-second breather, we restrain our natural impulse to start "doing something," and instead focus our attention directly on the customer. By doing so, our natural human instinct for reading visual cues is allowed to do its work, thus simplifying the whole selling process. Think about what we can see in front of us:

Basic physical characteristics—Some simple observations of size, proportion, body type, and skin tone should tell us what merchandise we have in stock that will work best for this customer and alert us to any special challenges in terms of fit, color, or style. A professional salesperson should never need to ask a size. The answer is right in front of you.

Appearances—What does the customer's clothing style, age, or gender tell us? While we'd never judge a book solely by the cover, it's unlikely that the black-clad, 22-year-old with a nose ring is looking for a blue blazer with brass buttons. The 50-year-old businessman at Sephora is not browsing. He's buying a gift and he needs help as soon as he can get it. As any good film director knows, one good visual image tells more than a dozen lines of dialogue. You can often read the whole story of someone's situation in one quick, establishing shot.

Body language—In the same way, like the actors that we are, we all convey clear messages through simple gestures and even just our pace of movement. It doesn't take a private detective to surmise that a woman glancing at her watch is in a hurry. A person that goes directly to a specific part of the store is (a) probably looking for something in particular and (b) familiar enough with our store to know his or her way around.

Group dynamics—Watch a group of friends shopping together. It's usually easy to discern who is the ringleader, which friends are engaged in the activity, and which ones are just along for the ride. Likewise, observe the dynamics between husband and wife. If one spouse is tired and grumbling, we had better find a way to make him or her comfortable immediately—or the stay in our store will likely be short.

Clues To Conversation-Starters—Remember, step 1 is "Don't leap. Look." In only a few seconds, we're going to need to approach the customer and say something. Now is our moment to give it some thought. I will say it more than once in this tome, but here it is for the first time:

"Can I help you?" is not an acceptable opening line.

It fails on many levels, some of which we'll discuss shortly. But at the very least, it shows an appalling lack of imagination.

Consider this example:

A woman walks in our shop with two small children, as her husband trails behind, struggling with several large bags from a local toy store. It's snowing outside and the woman is wearing a purple scarf from our store. She has no umbrella and her bare hands are stuffed in her coat pockets to keep warm. The children are tugging at her sleeve, complaining of being thirsty…and the best opening line we can muster is, "Can I help you?" Please. Of course we can help. Let us count the ways:

The children—We could acknowledge the children, ask them about the new toys in their shopping bags, and perhaps offer something to drink.

The husband—We could acknowledge the load of shopping bags and offer to put them behind the counter so that he can browse more comfortably.

The woman—We could compliment her on the scarf and acknowledge that she is clearly familiar with the brand. We could mention the weather and suggest that she really should see the new gloves that match her scarf. We could suggest an umbrella in a complementary color.

When we approach a customer, we are not at the beginning of a story. We are entering a show already in progress. Our job is to acquaint ourselves with the customer's situation as quickly and unobtrusively as possible, then write ourselves into the script. All we have to do is key into small visual cues to uncover the information we need.

"Can I help you?" is the way one would greet a stranger. But someone is a stranger only at the moment they enter our world. If we restrain our impulse to leap and spend a few seconds truly looking at the profile in front of us, we should be able to approach our customers in a way that is genuinely friendly and that will put them immediately at ease. Most people are open books. We have to take a moment to read them.

DON'T TALK. *Listen*

Is there any more enduring stereotype of the salesman than that of the garrulous, blustering big-talker—full of information that's not asked for, social chitchat that's not welcome, and promises that can't be kept? Even with this nefarious Ghost of Salesmen Past haunting our every move, we still find ourselves thinking that if we could just come up with the right line...that perfect piece of persuasive information...the cute quip that wins over the heart and mind...

The truth is, we don't sell by talking. We sell by listening. Talking is merely a necessary evil to get customers to open up and share their questions, needs, or points of view. When we are talking rather than listening, it's as if we're taking target practice with our eyes closed—trying to put as many conversational arrows into the air as possible, with the vague hope that one might find the mark. The less we talk, the more we can learn, and the more likely it is that we can respond with the crucial bit of information that the customer needs to make their purchasing decision.

Let the OTHER fellow talk occasionally.
You can't learn much listening to yourself.

Now of course, there is an obvious fact that needs to addressed straightaway: We can't listen if the customer isn't talking. First things first. Something is probably going to have to be said in order to get the customer to enter into a dialog.

As we have seen, "Can I help you?" is not that thing. By asking a direct, yes-or-no question, we give ourselves at least a 50-percent chance (probably better) that the conversation will be over before it has begun. Ask a simple question; get a simple answer.

While "Can I help you?" is a pretty weak opening line, I have heard worse. How's this: "If you have any questions, let me know." Wow. Congratulations. There's an opening line that doesn't even require the customer to say "no." At least we can be assured of plenty of peace and quiet on the selling floor.

What if, instead, everything we said from the beginning of our transaction was designed to elicit more information? Any advertiser knows that an effective selling campaign grows naturally out of a solid understanding of the customer. You won't get that information by talking. You'll get it by listening.

Let's begin by asking open-ended questions. These are questions that will earn us not just a "yes" or "no," but some actual insight into what the customer wants and who the customer is. It's not so hard. It's the difference between "Can I help you?" and "*How* can I help you?"

Better yet, try:

> "*What brings you into the store today?*"

> "*What caught your eye?*"

Banal? A little. But a customer can't respond to it with a head nod, or a simple yes or no. They have to say something about themselves in order to answer the question. If they are looking for something in particular, this is clearly their opportunity to tell you. Their response might be:

> "*I like the green sweater.*"

> "*I'm looking for the new updated model.*"

> "*I'm here to make a return.*"

Okay. Not a wealth of information yet, but within each of these answers lies a potential conversation.

> *"We have that sweater right over here. Is green a favorite color or is this to go with a specific outfit?"*

> *"That model just came in. Which model do you have now? How do you like it?"*

> *"I can make the return for you. What about the product didn't work for you?*

If we are listening well to the response, we should be able to glean something of the customer's color preferences and wardrobe needs, or their previous history with our products, or their likes and dislikes about the product they purchased. To a marketer, this would be valuable information. At the very least, it opens the door to a dialogue and a chance either to build on a potential sale ("Have you seen the green scarf?") or perhaps turn a return into an exchange ("I can understand why that one didn't work, but I think this might be exactly what you're looking for...").

Of course, the above examples are pretty easy ones. None of the hypothetical customers are exactly chatterboxes, but at least their answers are pretty straightforward. What about the more evasive, or even downright negative, responses?

> *"I noticed you just opened recently. I was kind of curious."*

> *"I'm really only killing time. Waiting for my wife..."*

> *"Trying to get out of the cold..."*

Not exactly hot prospects are they? But if we listen closely, there is still information to be gleaned.

> *"Yes, we opened last week. Do you live or work in the area?"*

> *"Sounds familiar. Is your wife getting her hair cut next door?"*

> *"I know—the weather is terrible. Are you in from out of town?"*

To listen well, we need to hear more than what's being said. All of the above responses require some degree of inference but are based on logical deductions. Someone who notices a new store opening is probably not a stranger to the neighborhood. Someone searching for refuge in rough weather is probably not a local.

Again, the key is to encourage dialogue by using open-ended questions, then picking up the clues that will allow the conversation chain to continue. Note the pattern in each exchange. First, we listen to what the customer has said. Then, we offer a statement affirming our understanding of what we heard. Finally, we follow with another question (open-ended if possible) to build upon what we've learned.

SETTING: A housewares store. Mainstreet USA.

A weary-looking man trudges in; checks his watch. Picks up a new slicer-dicer gadget. Gives it a quick once-over and sets it down again.

SELLER: Hello. What brings you into our store today?

MAN: *(not very interested)* Nothing specific.
I'm really only killing time. Waiting for my wife.

SELLER: Sounds familiar. Is she having her hair cut next door?

MAN: *(taking another glance around)* No. She's across the street with my daughter.

SELLER: Ah, at David's Bridal. Who's getting married?

MAN: My daughter. In June. They're shopping for a gown now. Thought I'd leave them to it.

SELLER: Of course. Some things are better left to the experts.
(Man is looking at a set of champagne flutes.)
With all the good news in the family, you may need a set of those.

MAN: Well, that's the truth. My son and his wife just had a baby. My first grandchild. Going to visit them tomorrow.

SELLER: Congratulations. Where are they living?

MAN: Upstate—that's where we're all from.
We're just down here for a day of shopping.

Okay. You get the point. Someone wanders in, and in less than 50 words, we've obtained a relatively thorough customer profile with a few casual questions, some adept listening, and a bit of logical inference. Even better, we have several sales opportunities staring us in the face: bridal registry and children's furnishings, in particular. "Can I help you?" would not have gathered this information. Neither would a two-minute dissertation on the virtues of the slicer-dicer gadget. The key was in listening and in building upon each new bit of information.

As we can see from the above example (or as any parent or psychoanalyst could tell us), sometimes listening is hard work. This is one of the best things about it. Because it requires so much concentration, the act of listening will usually ensure that we don't talk too much. It will also keep our concentration focused firmly on the customer and not ourselves or on other distractions in the store.

Best of all, listening is an investment in our future. It is an action that distinguishes the professional salesperson from a clerk. The business of selling is all about moving someone from customer to client. The only way to do this is through gathering information. If we've gathered no information during the transaction, a customer that has purchased from us is still merely a stranger with a sales receipt. No matter how many people we persuade to buy our product, we will never have a clientele until we begin to listen.

"Good listeners make more SALES than good talkers."

DON'T TEACH. *Learn*

Product information is like a hammer. Wielded correctly, at the right time and place, we can use it to hit the nail on the head. But if we start swinging it around indiscriminately, there's a good chance we'll bludgeon the customer into a stupor. People are interested in information that is *relevant* to them. The rest of it registers like the voices of the parents in *Charlie Brown's Christmas*: "Wah, wah, wah..."

Have you noticed that the descriptions of the daily specials at restaurants seem to be getting more and more involved? No longer are we simply told what the fish of the day is. We are now treated to a full description of where it came from, how it will be prepared, what it will be served on, what type of seasonings will be used, the degree to which the chef prefers to cook it, and the kind of wine suggested to accompany it. Good thing that so many waiters are also actors. No one else could memorize this stuff.

Of course, if we don't want fish, all of the information is irrelevant. Even if we do have a hankering for fish, we're probably only listening to part of the description and then keeping an ear open for any information that might turn us off to that particular dish. Another person at the table may have food allergies. They're listening primarily to hear mention of anything that might be dangerous for them. The point is: we are all listening through our own prism of self-interest.

As sellers, we need to learn what each customer's needs, priorities, motives, or concerns are—then provide the information relevant to that particular customer. What will he or she use the product for? Is it more important that it be stylish or functional? Does the customer prefer something technologically innovative or simple and easy to use? Is price a factor? Where will he or she be using the product? What is the ultimate objective of the purchase?

If we can answer these questions, we immediately know what information will be of interest to this customer. We are not leading a tutorial. Any information we offer should engage the buyer directly at his or her own point of interest. We can then work backward, filling in any gaps of knowledge or addressing any concerns. If we look and listen effectively, we will learn what criteria the customer is applying to his or her purchase decision. No amount of product knowledge will help us until we know what matters to the person with whom we're speaking.

We would do well to ask ourselves after each interaction, "Who learned more, the customer or me?" If the customer gained more knowledge about the product than we gained about the customer, then we probably taught more than we learned. And we probably saddled the customer with more information than he or she needed. Remember: the customer wants to leave with a shopping bag, not a diploma. We need to learn who we're talking to, how they live and work, what they need from the product, and what concerns they have about the purchase. Then and only then can we tell them what they really need to know.

DON'T LEAD. *Follow*

When it comes to traveling, I'm not a big fan of guided tours. I know all the arguments in favor of them: they provide a good general overview; you learn more; it's a more organized approach to sightseeing. But, it doesn't matter whether the guided tour is in a museum or a new town; there's something about me that resists the structure of it. I'm an explorer. Show me a door marked "Do Not Enter" and I'm irresistibly drawn. The problem with a guided tour is that wherever the tour guide has decided *not* to take me is precisely where I want to go.

But then I imagine this: What if I could wander wherever I wished? What if, when I found something of interest, I could turn to a knowledgeable friend who would tell me something about what I'm seeing, suggest a couple of related things I might want to visit, and take me there if I get lost? Instead of feeling led, I would feel like a leader. Rather than resisting the information being offered to me, I could embrace it because it's related to something in which I have a direct interest. It's the difference between a grade school field trip to the art museum and a private viewing with the museum's curator.

It's not hard to find the shopping equivalent of the guided tour. We've all had experiences in which the salesperson insists on showing us an endless array of items in which we have no interest. Usually, the motivation is unstated but obvious. The things we're being shown are:

- expensive
- overstocked
- a special promotion

As the customer, we know immediately that we are being led down the proverbial garden path. The danger signs are up and our natural impulse is fight or flight.

Indeed, it's not only the customer who's at risk in this scenario. By taking the lead, the seller is also living dangerously. When we lead, our eye is on where we're going and not on the person behind us. We're like the sightseeing guide who rushes on to the next statue in the piazza, then turns to find his tour group has meandered off to the café or the postcard shop. By stepping in front of the customer, we've lost sight of them. Our focus has turned to our own objectives and ourselves.

If our true goal is to learn about the customer, we can gather much more information by following. By allowing the customers to set the pace, we can see whether they are hurried or browsing. By watching what items catch their eye, we can determine where their interests lie. By listening to their comments, we can pick up clues about their lifestyle. By welcoming their questions, we can understand their priorities. Armed with that knowledge, we can then make suggestions that are proactive, without being p—

Gasp! So many sellers live in terror of the "p" word. In any sales skill or clientele meeting I've led, the explanation for any number of selling miscues is the same: "We don't want to be *pushy*." The stereotype of the pushy salesperson is so pervasive that a whole generation of sellers now prefers to avoid any sales approach at all, rather than run the risk of being too forward. We would do well to remember that "passive" is a "p" word too.

The fact is, we are only pushy when we're trying to sell someone something they don't want or force a decision that they are not ready to make. No one is annoyed by a seller who shares a little information about a product in which the customer has an interest. (Remember, I said "a little." *Don't teach. Learn.*) Most people are not offended by a suggestion based on an intelligent reading of their needs or tastes. In fact, they welcome it. Someone trying to help us work through a decision is not uncomfortable. Someone trying to hurry us ahead is.

The line is clearly drawn. Only when we lead rather than follow the customer do we risk stepping over the boundary between attentive and annoying. If we allow the customer to set the direction, determine the areas of interest, and reach a decision in his or her own time, we can be as active as we like without risking offense. It's all a matter of positioning ourselves properly—behind, not in front of, the customer.

Of course, sometimes a customer wants to be led. Watch the men in a jewelry store on Christmas Eve and you'll see an army in desperate search of a general. Fine. We've been given an invitation and we can comfortably take command. This is a golden opportunity—not to mislead, but to seize the opening for conversation, interaction, information gathering, and trust building. To meet someone who is lost and lead them to their destination is to lay the foundation for a long-term relationship. If you come through on Christmas Eve, Valentine's Day is only eight weeks away.

But what if the customers don't know they are lost? They think they know where they're going, but they're headed in the wrong direction. What then? I know, I know…the customer is always right, you say. I'm not so sure about that. Grab your own photo album from ten years ago. How right were those clothing choices? Clearly, there are moments when we are not best left to our own judgment. Could we as buyers sometimes benefit from a little subtle redirection?

Again, the tour guide analogy is probably apt. Most of us do not enjoy being led by the nose along a route that does not interest us. But if we obliviously wander toward the edge of a cliff, most of us would appreciate a gentle word of warning from someone more knowledgeable of the terrain. This is not "leading." This is commonly known as "helping."

A seller who is interested in building a clientele must learn how to allow a customer to explore on his or her own, while protecting that same customer from lapses in judgment, gaps in product knowledge, or the crazy whims of fashion. It's not always easy. The experienced seller knows that sometimes there's just no protecting people from themselves. But if we can find that magic balance, there is a reward for our careful efforts. That is the seller's equivalent of the Holy Grail:

TRUST. If we can allow the customer to lead but also instill in them the confidence that we are not going to let them wander into the quicksand, we have accomplished something far greater than simply closing a sale. We have established a foundation of trust upon which we can build an enduring relationship.

In the end, there is one single element that distinguishes whether we are leading a customer, or helping them. We know it and, in most cases, the customer will know it as well. It is all a question of where our "I" is. Is this transaction about us or the customer? Ultimately, what is our motivation?

DON'T SELL. *Serve*

This may be the first book devoted to selling that offers that advice. For those who make our living selling, it makes us a little nervous, doesn't it? It probably makes our employers a little nervous as well. After all, we're not working for a public service organization. We get paid to sell.

But the customer pays for service. Herein lies the paradox. We want to sell, but no customer enjoys being "sold." The customer wants to be helped. The more motivated we are by the desire to make a sale, the more at odds we are with the customer and the more likely we are to encounter resistance. On the other hand, the more motivated we are by the desire to serve the customer's needs, the more in sync we are with the customer. Thus, we find it easier to develop a relationship and ultimately, yes, make a sale. We do well by doing good. And that's good business.

Does this seem strange? Perhaps. But our lives are full of things that can be accomplished only by reaching for something else. Have you ever been befriended by someone whose motivation is solely to have more friends? A little scary. Have you ever met someone whose primary motivation is to be "happy"? How happy did they seem? Some things in life we can accomplish by setting the target and keeping our efforts focused firmly on the prize. But many things, particularly those based on interactions with others, can be accomplished only by aiming somewhere else entirely. We set off for one destination and arrive at another on our way.

Again, it is all a matter of what we have our "I" on. If our motivation is self-centered, it will be difficult to accomplish anything that requires social interaction. If our goal is to sell more, have more friends, and be happy, we will encounter resistance all along the way. Most people are not eager simply to be steppingstones on the road to our personal self-fulfillment. But when our motivation is to help customers, provide excellent service, and ensure that the customer is satisfied, *voila*! Suddenly, we sell more, make some friends, and find ourselves feeling very…well, happy.

Okay, it all feels a bit Zen, right? Maybe it sounds a little too cuddly for the working world. Yet we know that many companies have embraced this idea, at least in theory. Companies have "service standards," "service awards," "service initiatives," and "service pledges." They reward employees for "outstanding service" and build customer service departments. Nothing sells—and keeps on selling—like service, because it builds a committed clientele.

With all this emphasis on service…where is it? Have you seen it? Me neither. Despite all the corporate initiatives, I suspect that most consumers would say that service is getting worse, rather than better. Make a trip to your local mall and try to make a simple return. Why has all the zeal for keeping the customer happy not filtered down to the selling floor, which is where the customer happens to be?

I suspect that much of it comes down to motivation. We know that many companies' customer service initiatives are aimed more at public consumption than toward inspiring the workforce. Even the creation of a customer service department, separate from the "selling" division, sometimes feels a bit like the separation of church and state, or keeping the lions from the lambs. It's as if the two ideas, customer service and selling, somehow don't quite belong together.

THE *smile* ON THE FACE OF SOME SALESPEOPLE OFTEN REMINDS ME OF THE TOP LAYER OF APPLES IN A BOX, OR BERRIES IN A BASKET.

A genuine motivation toward customer service recognizes that selling and service are inseparable. They are two sides of the same coin. No one is an effective seller unless he or she can cultivate a clientele; customers will not become clients unless they believe that a seller is genuinely concerned with serving their needs. Any corporate commitment to service must begin on the selling floor. It does not begin after a sale has been made. Service begins the moment the customer enters the store.

The good news is, it's generally easier to serve than to sell. Persuading a customer to buy something they don't want is very tough sledding indeed. Helping a customer find what they do want is usually much easier. We don't have to be clever, just clear. We don't have to be persuasive, just perceptive. Most of all, we don't need to be aggressive, just efficient.

But we must be in it for the long haul. Unlike Houdini the 30-Second Seller, we can't perform a disappearing act upon the sound of the cash register's "*ker-ching!*" At the point of sale, our work has just begun. Our willingness and ability to follow through will determine whether this selfless approach to selling is an effective means of building a business or a shining example of "nice guys finish last."

If we have created a relationship of trust with the customer, then we have laid the foundation for building a clientele. Good for us. But violating that trust by failing to provide the expected service will undo all of that work. The devil truly lies in the details. Deliveries must arrive on time. Packaging must be up to standard. The product must perform as promised. Any problems, real or perceived, must be immediately and graciously resolved. The customer must be recognized and acknowledged.

Whether it's a sale, a return, a complaint, or a special request, each interaction with the customer is a test in which the customer will confirm the seller's true motivation. Is the seller in it for the customer or the seller? There is an opportunity in every aspect of every transaction either to reaffirm our commitment to our clients, or to reveal that our relationship extends only as far as their credit cards will take them.

This is why I find it puzzling that so many sellers avoid customers who are making returns, exchanges, or complaints. Here is a tailor-made opportunity to demonstrate our commitment to service. In many ways, it's easier to begin a conversation with someone making a return than to approach a casual browser. At least in these situations, the customer has a very obvious need. If we can address the concern gracefully, we will instantly build a level of trust that might otherwise take months to develop.

Just as difficult circumstances so often breed the strongest friendships, clientele relationships often grow out of interactions with customers who have problems that need solving. A customer does not need to be a buyer to become a client. If our goal is truly to serve, then any customer who needs help is a potential client. Whether or not the relationship develops profitably will depend largely on the quality of service we provide.

DON'T THINK. *React*

At this point, we should all be starting to relax a little. In case you haven't noticed, this process of getting the "I" out requires us to do less, not more. All of the pressure of trying to persuade, push, and ply the customer into submission is lifted. Instead, we're free to converse and cooperate for the greater good—that is, the customer's, not our own. It sounds easy…maybe too easy. That's precisely the point. We are taking the path of least resistance. So if our interactions feel smoother, even effortless, we're doing something right. There is no "A" for effort.

I'm not a big fan of sports analogies. Unlike my husband, who seems to find the answer to the most complex issues of our time revealed in the X's and O's of locker-room chalk talk, I don't find the spectacle of guys in shorts chasing a bouncing ball to be an apt metaphor for life. But I'm going to make an exception, just this once. And here it is: Selling is like baseball. Not football.

Too often, we treat selling like football. We try to pummel the customer into a purchase. The sales staff is exhorted to treat each new walk-in the way a 300-pound lineman pursues a quarterback. We try to fight through objections, block attempts to flee, and finally, force the desperate customer into surrender. The action is fast and furious, and any resulting carnage is all part of the game.

What if, instead, we approached each interaction the way that Derek Jeter steps into the batter's box? We would be cool, confident, and deliberate, focusing our attention on the customer as we wait for him or her to toss the ball toward the plate. Then, we would see the pitch and respond, waiting until the perfect moment…and finally swinging with split-second timing to meet whatever's been thrown at us. Our selling success lies not in our ability to initiate action, but in our ability to respond to action—not to act, but to *react*.

Now don't get the wrong idea. Just because a great ball player can make hitting a ball look effortless, we shouldn't assume that there is no work involved. Likewise, what appears to be a simple sales transaction can demand a Herculean effort from the seller. But in this game of selling, most of the heavy lifting is done off the field. We strategize and prepare, gather information about the customer, learn about our product, and hone our approach.

Then, as the transaction begins, we try to relax, focus our concentration, and trust our instincts to react to the unique demands of each customer. The key is to take our time but not to miss the moment—to see where the customer is headed and go there instantly. Through it all, the great sellers never let you see them sweat.

As we'll see in the next two sections, *Taking the "I" Out of Clientele* is not a lazy man's approach to selling. In the next section, "Moving the 'I' Back Where It Belongs," we'll see just how much we need to learn about a customer before we can consider them a client. Then, in the final section, we think about "Putting Our 'I' Into Action." There, we'll find enough work to fill our days and probably our evenings as well. This is a professional's approach to selling. It requires the same amount of energy and devotion that other professionals invest in their careers. As sellers, we should know that nothing comes for free.

Within the selling transaction itself, our goal should be a kind of effortlessness, born of preparation and practice, but invisible to the customer and even to ourselves. By following the Don'ts and Do's of Selling, we remember to keep our "I's" right where they belong: on the client. If our "I's" are in the right place, our reactions will not lead us wrong.

Now that we've managed to get ourselves out of the picture, we can begin to truly see the person standing in front of us. Simple as it seems, many sellers never make it to this point. Our next step is to begin to understand the person we're looking at. The difference between customers and clients is not how much they buy. It's how well we know them. Let's get acquainted…

MOVING *the* "I" BACK WHERE *it* BELONGS

IN·TEL·LI·GENCE

in·tel·li·gence Pronunciation Key (n-tl-jns) *n.* (1a.) The capacity to acquire and apply knowledge, especially toward a purposeful goal. b.) The faculty of thought and reason. c.) Information; news about specific or timely events. d.) Secret information, or the operation of gathering such information. e.) The ability to comprehend; to understand and profit from experience
(The American Heritage Dictionary)

Now there's an "I" word anyone can love. After all, it can mean so many different things in different situations. To James Bond, it's all about gathering information—bits of knowledge large and small that can provide a picture of a particular subject. To Stephen Hawking, it might refer to the ability to infer and interpret the knowledge that we have. To Jack Welch or another corporate CEO, it probably means something a bit more practical: good judgment, that magic combination of intuition, instinct, and information that leads to effective action.

So what does it mean to us?

SEARCHING *for* SIGNS
OF *Intelligent Life*
IN THE *Selling* UNIVERSE

Not always easy to find, is it? Caught in the chaos of the selling floor, buffeted by the irrational exuberance of our best customers and the impatience of our worst, it's tempting to accept ourselves as hostages to fortune. They come, they buy—we stack 'em high and let 'em fly. Some days we win, some days we lose, some days we stay open 'til 9. *Que será, será.*

I'm always nervous when a store manager ends a discussion of sales goals with an addendum like, "We're really hoping things turn around next week. We'll do our darndest...." Likewise, I'm never reassured when a sales associate refers to a bad "run" of luck. These are not the descriptions of a rational universe. These phrases indicate that we have surrendered to the Dark Side, where anything can happen at any time for any reason—and often does. In an environment like this, no one reads books about effective selling strategies. They put on their lucky ties and hope for the best.

"...AND WHAT IS THAT, JOHN? WHAT? BAD LUCK. THAT'S ALL IT IS. I PRAY IN YOUR LIFE YOU WILL NEVER FIND IT RUNS IN STREAKS. THAT'S WHAT IT DOES, THAT'S ALL IT'S DOING. STREAKS. I PRAY IT MISSES YOU. THAT'S ALL I WANT TO SAY."
Shelly Levine, GLENGARRY GLENROSS, *by David Mamet*

But we are thinking people and we know that there is an underlying order to things. Despite what it may look like in the mall on a Saturday afternoon, there is some kind of logic operating, even if it's often kept under the counter and shown only upon request. Some people win consistently, others lose consistently, and some stores sit empty while others are full. "Luck of the draw" is not an intelligent explanation.

Certainly, the corporations and entrepreneurs that create and operate the companies for whom we work understand this. Businesses are not built on a wing and a prayer. Markets are analyzed, locations are scouted, products are designed, and customers are targeted. Information is gathered, interpreted, and applied; intuition and intellect are combined to initiate action. Ask a brand's marketing director what's wrong with the business, and he or she will offer a description of demographics, or merchandise balance, or a price point comparison. Ask the same question at a meeting of the sales staff and too often you'll hear that it's been raining a lot lately.

A friend of mine in store management recently had to counsel a sales associate about her declining numbers. Five years ago, she had been one of the organization's strongest sellers. Why, my friend asked, had her productivity been declining over the past three years, even as the company as a whole had seen increasing sales? She shrugged. "Well, you gotta take the bad with the good," she replied. Lately, she concluded, she'd just had a nasty streak of luck.

Ah, but my friend is pretty sharp. He's been a seller himself so he can sense when someone is in danger of crossing over to the Evil Empire of Irrationality. He asked her: what about the success she had five years ago? Should that be attributed to luck as well? Was there no talent involved in what she had accomplished in those years?

If we wish to be recognized as skilled professionals, then we must accept that we operate in a rational (or at least somewhat rational) world. Our actions have consequences, and our results are related to our strategies and levels of effort. When things are coming up roses, we can enjoy the winner's bouquet with justifiable pride. When our efforts die on the vine, we know that our failure is understandable and correctable. As a former boss once told me, "Young lady, hope is not a strategy." We can't change the weather. There is much that is beyond our powers, but we do have one thing that distinguishes us from the other animals in the jungle, and the clerks at the local Mini-Mart:

Intelligence.

Intelligence is our stock in trade. It is our insurance policy against the ebb and flow of business cycles, foot traffic, and—yes—even luck. It's also our long-term job security plan, guaranteeing us that we will always have employment opportunities, no matter what happens to the store we're working for at any particular time. Taking the "I" Out of Clientele is the thinking person's approach to building a business, upon the four pillars of Intelligence:

(1) Identity—Knowing who our customer is.

(2) Information—Knowing what our customer is like.

(3) Interests—Knowing what our customer likes.

(4) Inventory—Knowing what our customer has liked in the past.

We must embrace intelligence in every sense of the word. With our "I's" firmly focused on the customer, we can sleuth like Sherlock Holmes, patiently gathering puzzle pieces of information about our clients until a portrait begins to emerge. Or we can play Socrates and ponder the greater meaning hidden in the data. We will not speak of luck, fate, or the possibility of rain.

So take out your pencils, and let's open our client books to page 1.

"Never mind the OUTLOOK for business.
Be on the LOOKOUT for business"

MOVING *the* "*I*" BACK WHERE *it* BELONGS: *on the* CLIENT

You do have a client book, don't you? Tell the truth. If you do, you are already a step ahead of most of the associates on your selling floor. I've found that usually only 20 to 30 percent of a sales staff has taken even this small first step toward building a clientele.

If one aspires to write the great American novel, the purchase of pencil and paper would be a wise, if inglorious, place to begin. Likewise, if we wish to build a clientele, we'll need a place to write some names. If someone claims to keep a clientele book in his or her head, this person either has a very small clientele, or the kind of mind that belongs on a television quiz show. We are going to be amassing a considerable amount of detailed information about the people who find their way onto our client lists. I strongly suggest that we write it down.

Where and how we write it down is up to us. During the course of my career, I have known a great many sales associates in a wide variety of selling environments. Strangely, almost all of them use a similar format for their client books. Some things just work. Most successful sellers keep their clients organized in a notebook or journal, with a full page allotted to each name. I'm not suggesting that this is the only way. If you prefer a computer file or a Rolodex, this is a matter of personal style. The only requirements are that the format be organized, easy to access, and expandable enough to accommodate our ever-growing amount of client knowledge. After all, this is a book with a beginning but no real end.

Wait. Did I hear something from the gallery? Was that a low rolling murmur of discontent? I thought I recognized the sound. Having worked with sales associates for more than 20 years in this particular area, I'm still surprised by the initial resistance to clientele development from the very people that it's supposed to benefit.

Objection #1: We don't have time for all this paperwork.

Of course we don't. There are customers waiting and there is stock replenishment to complete and shipping arrangements to be made and inventory counts to be done. Right? Our day is stuffed with necessary tasks, most of which must be attended to in a timely fashion and most of which, when completed, will do absolutely nothing to help us reach our sales goal tomorrow and the day after that. Herein lies a fundamental rule of time management.

Our hours can easily be consumed by duties that are necessary but not, in fact, highly productive. Necessary duties are things that must be done immediately but don't yield much in the way of long-term benefits. Let's call them "urgent but unimportant" tasks. At the same time, there are things that we could be doing that are not particularly urgent, but which would be of significant long-term benefit. These go in the "important but not urgent" category. Like weeds in a flower garden, the urgent but unimportant duties, if left uncontrolled, will inevitably squeeze out the time that should be allotted to the important but not urgent tasks. The result is a daily schedule of ever-increasing activity but decreasing productivity. We're doing more but accomplishing less.

Clientele development does not take time. It makes time. By forcing us to gather information and insight about our customers, the clientele development process constantly redirects our energy from the short-term tasks to a long-term investment in our future. If we sell to ten customers in a day but take no names, compile no information, and establish no relationships, tomorrow we begin right back at square one. Every hour of every day of every year, we're forced to start all over again.

But if we invest a few minutes in each transaction to convert even a portion of those ten customers into potential clients, we have made tomorrow and the next day just a little bit easier. We are building a base of customers to call upon when faced with selling challenges. When the fall shipment arrives, we can easily access our clients and invite them in to shop. When our manager challenges us to contact our customers about a specific event, we can immediately narrow down our list to the most viable prospects. Without greatly increasing our daily activity, we can significantly increase our productivity.

It's all a matter of minutes. Do we have five minutes between transactions to make notes on the customer that we just helped? Could we spare ten minutes of our lunch break to enter a new client in our book? Perhaps we could take 30 minutes at home one evening to review our sales receipts and update a client's inventory? Every professional has a stack of work that can't always be completed within working hours. This is why briefcases were invented. Occasionally, we can use some of our own time to finish those important but not urgent duties. If those tasks allow us to become more productive, then we have made a wise investment.

Objection overruled. The format is up to you, but the principle is non-negotiable. Let's make a list of our consistent customers and, by applying a bit of focus and, yes, even a little intelligence, attempt their transformation into clients. All "I's" are on the customer. But what are we looking for? Leave plenty of room. We're going to have a lot to write down next to each name.

IDENTITY-
"Just the Facts Ma'am"

The client's name? "Ah yes, the name. Well, you know…I'm not so good with names. Never forget a face. But names—they're a bit trickier, aren't they?"

They sure are. That's why we write them down. While it's impressive that we can place a face from two years ago, it's difficult to call someone a client if we don't even know his or her name.

In fact, it's difficult to call them at all. This is precisely the problem. We can't pick up the telephone and call a face. Nor can we mail to a physical description. I once worked with a sales associate who chased after a customer, yelling "Size 12, Size 12," because she didn't know the customer's name, only her size. This is not a good strategy. Particularly when it comes to the larger sizes. The reason we're creating a client book is so that we can easily be in contact with our regular customers. And there is only one way to do that:

We need a name. We need an address. We need a phone number. These are the basics. They are basics not because they're simple. They are basics because they're essential. Think of them as the "must haves" of our selling season. Nothing fancy here, just enough to establish identity. Remember, there is a multimillion dollar industry built on this information. It's called direct mail. There's a lot you can do with a name and address. But you have to get it first.

How is it that a sales associate who moments earlier was discussing whether a skirt made the customer's thighs look fat can find it "just a little too personal" to obtain a name and phone number? Yet this is the major stumbling block faced by most sellers when it comes to clientele. How can we get the customer's essential information without drawing perilously close to that dreaded "p" word. We don't want to be "pushy".

"Ah, so now we get to the sleuthing…" Surely this is the moment to devise some sly, covert method of tricking the customer into divulging this highly confidential information, right? So what's our secret plan?

Well, we could just ask. Maybe we say something terribly clever, like, "I know you're interested in that particular item. I'd like to be in touch with you when we receive the new shipment. Let me take your name and phone number and I'll be in contact with you next week."

Not exactly something out of John le Carré, is it? But this direct approach has several benefits. First, more often than not, it works. Assuming we have provided good service and established some rapport, most people will not hesitate to provide us with their contact information. Second, if the customer reacts negatively to this direct request, it lets us know immediately that even if we have made a sale, we have not succeeded in laying the groundwork for a relationship. Our test results are in: selling skills need improvement.

Or we may learn that this customer is open to a relationship but is highly protective of his or her privacy. Again, this is useful information. Now we know that this relationship will have to function within very limited parameters, which we must always respect.

The direct query is our greatest time management tool. When customers decline our requests for name and address, they are telling us in very clear terms that they are not prospective clients. Perfect. Now we can move on immediately, instead of spending months trying to cultivate a relationship with someone who is not interested in our product. It's a little like speed dating. There are a million fish in the ocean. Best to identify the cold ones quickly.

You'll find that most people will not say "no," however. Do you know why? Let's look again at the way we formulated our question:

"I know you're interested in that particular item.
I'd like to be in touch with you when we receive our new shipment."

Aha. This is the crucial bit. It all goes back to what our "I" is on. The phrasing of our question indicates that our focus is on helping the customer. We are serving, not selling. If we let customers know immediately how it will benefit them, we have every reason to believe that they will want to provide their contact information. Who wouldn't?

It's a simple matter of telling them why we want to know. Do we just want to add another entry to the list of names in our book? Or are we hoping to keep the customer apprised of new shipments, upcoming sales, items to complement what he or she has bought previously, or store events? The carrot can be customized to the customer, depending on where his or her interests lie. But we should never feel uncomfortable asking for the must-have clientele information. After all, we're providing a service that benefits not just ourselves, but the customer as well. So let's begin our client book by listing the must-have information:

- Name
- Address
- Phone number

Jot that down in your little black book. Who knows? This could be the start of a beautiful relationship...

INFORMATION-
Getting to Know You

The good news is, the toughest part is over. If we've managed to get the must-have information from the client, we have sketched the outline of our subject on paper. The rest is just filling in the details. Add enough detail and the picture of a real human being begins to take shape.

It won't (and shouldn't) happen all at once. Gathering a complete picture of your customer in one transaction would leave the poor shopper feeling like he or she had been grilled by Anderson Cooper on the way to the cashwrap. But with the right blend of observation and conversation, we can gradually begin to fill in the blanks in our client's portrait. We just have to look, listen, and learn.

Then we have to write stuff down. As we've already seen in some examples, even a casual conversation can tell us quite a story. The problem is that unless we write it down, the information will be lost to us as quickly as we can greet the next customer. We're trying to develop a profile here—and each bit of detail is another piece in the puzzle. Handle it with care.

With apologies to Dashiell Hammett...

A RED-LETTER DAY

She walked in near closing time, in a red dress that could stop traffic. "Size 6, and no room to spare," I noted, jotting it down in my dog-eared notebook that I keep for just such encounters. I'd seen this dame plenty of times before and sold her a ruby necklace just weeks ago. She bought it for the opera—but she didn't get it for a song. A slow day was suddenly heating up.

"Mrs. Kowalsky, what a pleasure. How did things work out for Pagliacci last week?" I asked. "Sam, what a remarkable memory. Let's just say that little bauble you sold me hit more high notes than the tenor did." I grinned. The old book had made me look good once again. I could see her relax as she approached my display case.

"I bought this little frock to match the ruby," she said. "What do you think?" What I really thought was that I had some ruby earrings just aching for a good home. But it was too early for that.

"Not around here you didn't. Must have been at some shop on Rue le Jour." This lady had more addresses than a city map—country homes, beach getaways, and a little pied-á-terre in Paris. Luckily, I had the only number that mattered: a cell phone that reached her anytime, anywhere. Right there in my Golden Book.

"How did you guess? I was there last week. But when I got your call, I couldn't stay away." "And you're back just in time for the Winter Auction," I added, knowing it was more than my new box of goodies that brought her back to town. Madame was a dealer in rare antiquities and never missed the auction. I had it marked in my calendar with a red "x," right next to her birthday. I've always had an eye for dates.

"Oh, there's more to it than that…" she replied, playing the mouse to my cat. But this was no game. A fresh tear escaped from behind her dark glasses. I was starting to get nervous. "It…it's Harold. He's coming back," she stammered. Now I was scrambling. I knew the husband's name was Fred, an insurance guy who worked downtown. The notes in my book were clear and the book never lied. Was I in over my head here?

Then I remembered the note scribbled in the margins, years earlier. She'd mentioned it only once in passing. There was a son, about 25, an archeologist who'd moved to the wilds of Guinea. They were close once but now there were issues. I decided to take a gamble. "From Africa?" I tossed out, with more confidence than I had a right to muster. "Yes," she replied. "He's getting married."

And now I could see, these were tears of joy—a mother's joy. I exhaled and turned the page in my notebook. "Harold," I wrote in the heading. Then I turned back to the mother of the groom. "Well, we do have some very nice engagement rings and wedding bands, if he'd like to take a look," I offered. "Why don't I give him a call when he gets into town?"

As any detective could tell us, the small details are sometimes the best clues. Each piece of information is another element in the chain, linked to what we already know and leading somewhere else at the same time. What holds it all together is our memory and the notes in our clientele book. So what does our inquiring mind want to know?

First, let's keep in mind that there is a difference between what we *need* to know and what we'd *like* to know. We already know three of our must-haves:

Name
A name says a lot: ethnic background, marital status, even professional position. And is it Robert, Bob, Dr., the Bobster? What is the preferred name? Make a note of it. It beats yelling "Size 12" across the selling floor.

Address/Phone Number
Remember the direct mail industry. It's an empire built on zip codes. Where someone lives gives important hints to lifestyle, income level, hobbies, and interests. Of course it's a generalization. But at least it's a start.

Previous Contact
We have to know when we've seen our customers and when we've last been in touch with them. This reminds us when we need to reestablish contact or warns us that we're overdoing it. It may reveal patterns in the times of year that they shop with us, how often they visit, and whether the visits are growing more frequent, or less.

Now let's get to the good stuff. Maybe we don't absolutely need to know it. But admit it. You're a little curious

Job
A job is more than a job. What someone does, or doesn't do, for a living can tell us about their interests, their lifestyle, their educational background, perhaps their daily schedule. They may be members of professional associations. They probably attend industry events. There's more to life than work. But most of us only dream of seeing it.

Physical Characteristics
It's no substitute for a name, but particularly if we're selling clothes, we need to keep a record of sizes and other physical traits. Height, approximate weight, hair or eye color, skin tone—it can all be relevant, depending on the product. If we sell eyeglasses, we should know someone's vision information. If we're selling shoes, keep a lookout for falling arches.

Family
Married or single? Parent? Daughter or son? Brothers and sisters? Grandchildren? We're talking gifts here, people. Which leads us to:

Important Dates
What are the big numbers in our client's life? If we sell someone an anniversary gift or something for the daughter's birthday, let's mark it down. It will come again next year.

Friends—Did someone recommend us to them? Have they sent friends to us? Do we know the social circle in which they travel? Networks aren't only on television. Every client has one. This is how we build our business.

Likes and Dislikes—William Stubbs, an interior decorator, wrote a book called *I Hate Red. You're Fired!* Sound familiar? Each of us has our preferences, our passions, and our phobias. They don't have to be rational. They're ours. But if someone is our client, we better know his or her hot buttons, for better and for worse. Mark them in red in your client book. Unless of course you hate red.

By now, we're hot on the trail and the pages in our client book are filling up quickly. The pieces of the puzzle are fitting together into an immediately identifiable portrait; our interactions with the customer are profitable and personalized. But there's still something missing from the picture. We have a plethora of information—but we're missing the passion. So let's get down to what really makes our client tick…

INTERESTS-
"The Secret Garden"

Now this is the way to the heart. It's not hard to tell the difference between some-one shopping for a gift and someone indulging his or her own interest. Whether it's the opera or the Super Bowl, cooking or mountain climbing, decorating a home or traveling the world, everyone has things that they're passionate about. If we can uncover one or two of these for each client, we'll be getting very close to a definitive portrait. Plus, we'll never be at a loss for conversation.

In fact, conversation is the key to unlocking this particular treasure box. Unlike the must-have information (name, address, phone number, contact record), direct inquiry is not the best way to discover someone's interests. If put on the spot, most of us stammer helplessly trying to describe what we're interested in. But if someone were to hit on one of those subjects in conversation, the light in our eyes would give us away immediately. Finding where someone's interest lies is not always an easy journey. But you'll know when you get there.

THERE'S *Information,* AND THERE'S *Infer-*MATION

So how do we get there? It's all a matter of information and "*infer*-mation." Let's start with what we know:

Address: Aspen, Colorado
Job: Sports agent
Phone: Cell phone only. Rarely in the office.
Physical characteristics: Tall, thin, physically fit.
Family: Wife and one young son.
Likes: Casual clothing, athletic attire, wears a sports watch, usually drives an SUV with a ski rack when he's with the family, or a motorcycle when he's on his own.
Dislikes: Suits and ties. Returned a set of cuff links last year as "too fussy."
Friends: Was referred by the manager of Aspen Highlands ski resort. Represents several former Olympic skiers. Member of Aspen Glen country club.

This is our information—carefully gathered and duly noted in our client book. Now let's add some "infer-mation" to round out the picture:

Likes the great outdoors. Probably a skier and a golfer. Probably a sports fan too—right, Sherlock? Spends time with athletes, many hours on the phone, and does plenty of traveling. This is a family man with an informal, active lifestyle. Likely a former athlete in college and is still physically active. Probably follows the Nuggets and the Broncos, the latest in wireless technology, and the newest models of off-road vehicles. The key words are "practical," "durable," "comfortable," and "casual." Cuff links didn't catch his fancy; neither will desk accessories, wing-tip shoes, or an eighteenth-century French gilt mirror.

A mass of generalizations, assumptions, and stereotypes? Certainly. No one is suggesting that we act on this "infer-mation" as if it's fact. But it opens the door to further inquiry.

All of these assumptions can be easily tested in casual conversation. The verbal response of the customer and the body language will inevitably tell us when we're onto something good. Infer-mation is a crucial tool to initiate a conversation and to spare the customer the ordeal of a lengthy inquisition. We can't rely simply on the facts that we know. We need to be able to put 2 and 2 together without the help of a cash register. Infer-mation gives meaning to our information. It's not enough to know "who" the customer is. We need to know *what* their interests are.

We also need to know that there are two meanings to the word "interest." Both are worth keeping an "I" on.

THERE ARE INTERESTS, AND THEN THERE ARE *Interests*

Of course, when we talk about a client's "interests," we're referring to things in which the client is interested: hobbies, collections, subjects of study, favorite places to visit. In the above example, we could say that our client's "interests" are likely to be sports, both as a spectator and participant, spending time with the family, and, if we buy into our "infer-mation," possibly a curiosity about tech gear or recreational vehicles.

Any of these interests could provide a whole set of selling opportunities, if we can make our product relevant. If we're selling books to this customer, we'll lead him over to the sports and recreation section. If we're selling real estate, we'll find a house with a family room and a yard that can accommodate a Wiffle-ball game.

But there is a second meaning to the word "interest." When we use phrases like "what's in our best interest" or "protecting our own interests," we are talking about something much deeper than our hobbies. In this sense, the word "interest" refers to what we deem as having ultimate value. When used this way, the word describes not just what we think is "interesting" but what we think is valuable. Our "interests" are quite literally what we live for.

Most of our purchases serve our "interests." We buy groceries because we have an abiding interest in eating. We buy a car because it is in our interest to have transportation. But why do we buy a specific kind of car? Now, that goes deeper. Is our interest in how it looks? The level of status it conveys? Its comfort or practicality? Its value in relation to the cost?

Everyone's buying decisions are informed by some kind of logic. But that logic only makes sense if we understand the individual's value system. A middle-aged corporate lawyer values a fine, jewel-encrusted pen because he feels it provides status and a sense of sophistication. He purchases the pen because it serves his "interests." For the same amount of money, the lawyer's younger brother buys a ripped up black leather jacket from a vintage store, because he thinks the jacket is "cool." A customer's perception of the "value" of a product is entirely based on that customer's "values." You can explain to me the merits of a fine cigar, but if I don't smoke, it's tough to close the sale.

For this reason, an understanding of a customer's core "interests" is the most valuable knowledge that we can obtain. Identity is essential but not terribly revealing. Information is helpful but superficial. Hobbies may change but core values rarely do. What does the customer value? Utility or status? Comfort or elegance? Pleasure or power? This is where his or her true "interests" lie.

Very few clients will directly articulate these kinds of "interests." Many can't define themselves in this way, even if they try. Many others define themselves misleadingly—they tell us what they think should be important to them, or what they want us to think is important to them. Even clients willing to share their true "interests" will only do so when we know them so well that it would hardly be necessary.

All of our knowledge about our clients' core values will come to us through infermation. By observing their buying patterns, learning about their lifestyle, and watching them in interaction with friends and family, we can begin to understand what they are really looking for.

If we can discover what truly matters to the customer, we can easily identify those items in our store that serve the customer's interest. Or we can properly position our product so that we highlight the qualities or features that appeal to that particular client. The customer at the car lot whose interest is status does not want to hear about which model gets the best mileage. But a customer seeking efficiency will certainly want that information. Everyone has an interest in something. We just need to know what it is. Then we need to demonstrate how our product can serve that interest.

If we can align our product with our customer's interests, it should never be difficult to close a sale, even at a very high price point. After all, we're selling the customer something that has "value." It can be challenging to articulate someone's value system in a way that fits neatly into our clientele book. But once we've found our clients' true "interests," we know what they are seeking in life. When we know that, all we have to do is show them what they need to get there.

"SHOW A MAN YOU'RE INTERESTED IN *his business,* **AND HE WILL SOON BE INTERESTED IN YOURS."**

INVENTORY - *You Can't Win if You Don't Keep Score*

Once we gather information, we just have to keep track of it all. From plumbing the depths of our client's soul, we now turn to the slightly more mundane task of bookkeeping. It's not to be underestimated.

Did you know that the earliest form of writing, the *cuneiform*, was invented primarily to record commercial transactions? Luckily, the Mesopotamians saved their sales receipts. These clay tablets are what historians and archeologists use to piece together the clues of a long lost world. All of the details and character of daily life are captured in the minutiae of these ancient business accounts.

Just imagine—one day, someone may discover our client books, buried in the detritus of a lost civilization. Careful study by historians will bring our clients miraculously back to life for a new generation, reconstructed through the knowledge of what they bought, when they bought it, and in what size.

Even today, there's no better selling tool than a careful inventory of a customer's past purchases. Knowing what someone has goes a long way toward learning who they are. More importantly, knowing what they have will inevitably tell us what they need.

I still remember my first brush with the concept of clientele. My father used to buy his suits at a small, neighborhood clothing store, where his father shopped as well. Picture a dark, wood-paneled emporium with a leather couch and the radio tuned to a football game. It was a place where a female face was something of a novelty. But I recall walking in with my mother and being greeted by name by an older gentleman in an elegant suit. No introductions necessary—it was as if he'd been expecting us.

"Well, Father's Day is coming up," my mother began, "and we were hoping you could help us. He's so hard to buy for." The salesman smiled (of course he did) and nodded with confidence. As he stepped behind the desk, he opened a leather-bound book that seemed to hold answers to all of the mysteries of the male species' shopping habits.

"Well, he just recently bought that new sports jacket. I think what he could really use is a shirt and sweater to go with it." And he was off. Soon, a sports coat that looked just like my father's new one was laid on the counter, along with pants identical to what he'd worn to the office that morning. Then the salesman began to show us various combinations of shirts and sweaters that might do the trick.

All of the confusion that usually accompanied shopping seemed remarkably absent. There were no uncertainties about size or style. This seller knew what cut the shirt should be, what kind of cuff and collar my father preferred. "Doesn't he already have something like that one?" my mother asked, pointing to one of the sweater choices. "Not exactly," our new friend replied. "He has one more like this," and he grabbed a sweater off the shelf, which did indeed look very close to one of my father's favorites. "I think he bought this one for his brother," he said, pointing to one of the other finalists on the table. "So let's take it out of the running."

Minutes later, the sale was closed and our quest was complete. As he bent over to hand me the shopping bags (big surprise, I've always liked carrying shopping bags), he asked conspiratorially, "Now what about Grandpa? He should get something for Father's Day, too, don't you think?"

This guy was good. But he was no genius. He had a book that told him what he needed to know and he acted intelligently upon it. The new sweater and shirt were promptly entered into the inventory of purchases under my father's name, probably with a note that it was bought by my mother for Father's Day (in case she forgot and thought to do the same thing for his birthday). Guess what? He also knew what my grandmother had bought for my grandfather's gift and he had the perfect tie to go with it. Success builds upon itself, like blocks into a building. But we have to put the pieces in place by keeping records of what we sell and to whom we sell it.

Little did I know that what I saw in the men's store that day was actually standard practice at many of the smaller boutiques in the neighborhood. There was a women's clothing store around the corner that undoubtedly had my mother's name in a similar (but bigger) book. This is what prevented two ladies from showing up at the same event in the same dress. Someone was keeping track of this stuff.

I certainly could not have known as a little girl that this type of client record would one day become as rare as one of those artifacts from a lost civilization. "Once there was a time when a salesman would remember the customer's name and even what he had sold them…"

Nothing could be easier. To maintain an inventory list of what we have sold someone does not require us to ask any probing questions. We steer well clear of the "p" word.

There's no sleuthing involved and no great insight required. Best of all, it can be done at any time—after work, before opening, immediately after the sale, or during lulls in traffic.

If we walked into the store where we made a recent clothing purchase, would the sales associate remember what we bought? Would the associate have any immediately accessible record of it so that he or she could remember it six months from now? Probably not. Simply by maintaining a thorough inventory of what was purchased by our clients (and when they purchased), we could elevate ourselves into the upper echelon of sellers. Keep an "I" on inventory and everything else will follow.

Like those sales scrolls from the ancient world, our client's inventory holds within it almost all of the details we need for a profile. It tells us what type of items our customer buys as well as their color and style preferences, budget, and shopping habits. It suggests what they might need, what new products might appeal to them, and what might be due for replacement. It allows us to build upon our successes by adding additional items that complement what we've already sold the customer. It also illustrates our areas for improvement—"Why does she buy all her furniture from us, but never her appliances?" It is a perfect sales tool, built entirely on information that we already have.

It's also a great way to boost our popularity. By maintaining a record of what the client has and what he or she might need, we are the gurus who hold the answer to that most unanswerable of questions: "What will we get Uncle Charlie for his birthday?" Parents, children, wives, husbands, significant others, secretaries, and business associates will all climb to the top of the mountain to consult us.

For the holidays, birthdays, and other special occasions, we become the nucleus around which the family and social circle revolve by making sure that our client receives what he or she wants with no fit problems, style issues, or duplications. Think of it: the holidays unmarred by ugly moments. ("Wow, it's great. I love it. Uh…what is it?," as Aunt Marge bursts into tears.) And, the spare closet is no longer full of hand-me-down gifts. All thanks to us and our client books. For this small service to humanity, we may take each name in our client book and multiply it by three or four, or however many generous friends or relatives each client might have. Imagine all the interesting people we'll meet.

THE ROVING "*I*"

There is an invisible force at work here and it's called "intelligence"—the gathering of knowledge for a specific purpose. The more we have, the better we will sell. Some of what we learn about our client will be simple and straightforward (name, address, telephone number). Some will be picked up in conversation and some will be inferred from what we already know. Some of this knowledge will be superficial, some will be mundane, and some will be as deep as the nature of our client's character.

Just as all of us are evolving, so will our knowledge be ever-changing, as clients move through different phases of their lives. If you don't think that people in general are especially interesting, then sales is probably not the best career choice for you. If you find people endlessly fascinating, then you've found your life's work.

The repository of all of this accumulated knowledge is our client book. This is what gives order to our client information and moves our knowledge from the abstract to the specific. We don't need to guess or remember; we can simply learn and know.

When our knowledge is written down in an orderly format, we can refer to it, build upon it, analyze it, and share it with other people. Could we keep it all in our heads? Of course. Theoretically, we could keep all of our personal banking information in our heads as well—withdrawals, deposits, loan payments, bank fees. But if it's too important to risk forgetting, we write it down. The knowledge of our customers is an accumulation of all our efforts during all of the hours we spend in the store. It's worth writing down.

When I'm called as a consultant to help sales associates develop their businesses, the first step I take is to review their client book. If we want to know what's right and wrong with our business, what we could do to improve our selling, what opportunities we might have right now, or what our future prospects look like, the answer is inevitably in the book, written in bold letters, right there between the lines.

One of the advantages to a written record is that it allows us to study patterns of behavior, rather than relying on anecdotes and general impressions. We can see when and how our clients shop with us, and what they usually buy. Likewise, we can see our own behavior—what we do well and what we consistently forget to do. It's not always pretty, but this is how we learn. The first function of gathering intelligence is to see things as they really are, not as we wish them to be.

The second function of intelligence is to make us do something. A client book full of "intelligence" about our customers won't change our commissions for the month. We have to do something with the information. Picture an eye, as it slowly scans across the room…moving from a focus on self…to a focus on the customer…and it's still moving…

The real definition of intelligence is the transformation of information into knowledge, and then at last into action. It's time for our "I" to move again. We all know where it's headed…

PUTTING our "I" into ACTION

PUTTING *our* "*I*" *into* ACTION

Lights, camera…

It all comes down to this. All of our selfless interest in the customer, our information-gathering, and our careful record-keeping is only setting the stage for the show to begin. It's now time to shine the spotlight on the actors and wait for something to happen. And that means…

ACTION!

As sellers, most of us are happiest when we're in the heat of the action, engaging the customer and building a sale. Putting Our "I" Into Action plays to our strengths, allowing us to use our natural energy and ambition in a strategic way, to build better relationships and bigger sales.

That's right—I said bigger sales. Make no mistake; this is the goal. Just as we can be too aggressive in making a sale at the expense of a client relationship, we can also be too passive, until the customer wonders if we're really interested in selling anything at all. I call this the **Undercover Salesman**, who dons 1,001 disguises to masquerade as social worker, personal confidant, museum guide, or technical adviser—rather than owning up to the fact that he or she really is on the floor to (*shhh!*) sell stuff.

"I MEAN, ALL I'M DOIN' IS *sellin'*. WHERE'S THE CRIME IN THAT?" *Ernest Tilly*, TIN MEN, *by Barry Levinson*

Selling is not an undercover job. If we are serving the customer's interests, we don't need to disguise our desire to sell. In fact, most customers find the Undercover Salesman a little disconcerting, as it suggests that there is something embarrassing about the transaction that's taking place. Our motivation is to help and serve. But our function is to sell.

In realizing that function, we must recognize that the first move begins with us. We cannot just wait for something to happen. We must be the active force in driving our sales. If "business is off," it's because we are. And we can remedy it—through action.

Here are four things we can do immediately to put our relationships and intelligence into action. None of the following are theoretical. None can be accomplished without some effort. But taken together, they will work. It's up to us to keep our noses to the grindstone and our "I's" on the prize. Items for our to-do list:

1. "I" Will Identify
2. "I" Will Initiate
3. "I" Will Individualize
4. "I" Will Increase

"*I*" WILL IDENTIFY
"*Many are Called. Few are Chosen.*"

Our first step in an "intelligent" approach to selling was defining our client's identity. The first step in putting our intelligence into action is identifying which customers are our "clients." Did you catch the difference? The former is something we discover. The latter is something we decide.

The identity of our customer is not up to us. Certainly, we need to take an active role in gathering the information, whether it's the must-have facts or the more revealing details of job, lifestyle, and personal preferences. But we can't create or recreate our client's identity. (If only!) Our role is simply to capture that information as accurately as possible in the pages of our client book. We are biographers—not novelists.

But as you, dear reader, could probably attest, every book needs some editing. That action is in our hands. We decide which characters get a page in our client book. We decide when someone should be added and when someone else should be dropped. Our first action is that of selection: identifying which customers are in our client book at any given time.

Hark. I hear the sound of thunder. Or maybe it's that rolling murmur of discontent once again…

Objection #2: But every customer is my client.

Or could be. Or has been. Or will be. We sellers are a hopeful lot, aren't we? I've found that there are two objections that sales associates have to the process of developing a client book. The first objection is starting one at all, as we have seen. The second objection is stopping. Seized by the thrill of making a list of our customers, many of us take it as a challenge to compile as many names as possible: people who shopped with us once, people who used to shop regularly with us, people who we hardly know but who seem awfully nice. The more, the merrier, right? Can't everyone be our client?

No. In the name of customer service, we should treat everyone *as if* they are our client. Indeed, everyone has the potential to be our client. But not everyone *will be* our client. Nor should they be. Our client book must be limited to people with whom we have an active ongoing relationship. As you'll see in the remaining pages, our approach to those who receive the hallowed title of Client will be active and aggressive, with an emphasis on direct personal interaction. It's not possible to take that approach with everyone. It will not be profitable to take that approach with just anyone. We must make some decisions.

This is what distinguishes the client book from a database. A database of names captured at the point of sale merely tells us who has purchased from us in the past. Our client book is forward thinking. It identifies those customers who we believe will purchase from us in the future. The database casts a wide net and drags up anything that's floating nearby. Our client book is a handpicked selection of the best business prospects we have. Sorry, Charlie. Not everyone qualifies. This party is reserved for people who we know and who know us—and who have an active interest in what we're selling.

In fact, that's a good criterion to start the process. If the person on page 1 of our client book walked into the store right now, would we recognize him or her? If we called the client on the phone, would he or she know us? Has the customer bought something from us in the past year? Has he or she expressed an interest in shopping with us in the future? If the answer is "yes" to at least two of the four questions, then we have a winner. Congratulations to our lucky shopper. They've earned a page in the story of our lives.

But if the answers to the above questions are predominately negative, then we need to make a cut. At the moment, this customer does not belong in our client book. Keeping his or her name on the roll will only divert our efforts, reduce our productivity, and drag down our results. It's time to say, "So long."

Don't panic. "So long" doesn't mean "goodbye." Like I said, we're a hopeful lot. Even the suggestion of removing a name from a client book often seems to send shivers down the spine of the most hardened sellers. Wouldn't want to do anything rash, would we?

Take them out of the ballgame. We don't need to eliminate them—just put them on the sidelines. Whether it's a paper file or a computer record, let's create a "holding station" for customers in limbo. These are people who haven't established themselves as clients according to our criteria, but who we're not quite ready to give up on, either. We will keep their information on hand, review it occasionally, and reach out to them when we have the right occasion. But we will not fool ourselves into believing they are clients.

Think of it as a kind of natural selection. Then, let's try to keep it natural. When we start identifying potential clients, we need to keep the process free from our own biases, hunches, and assumptions. If we have a "feeling", based solely on appearances, that someone is not a potential client, we may deliver a quality of service that ensures that our prophecy is fulfilled. The action of identifying clients is based on what we know, not on what we think.

In his book *Blink*, author Malcolm Gladwell offers a fascinating analysis of the danger of prejudging customers. He recounts the story of Bob Golomb, one of the most successful car salesmen in the Northeast. While many salesmen focus on pinpointing the patrons that appear to be the most lucrative, Golomb makes a point to filter out any consideration of a customer's appearance or likelihood to buy.

"Prejudging is the kiss of death," he says. "You have to give everyone your best shot. A green salesperson looks at a customer and says, 'This person looks like he can't afford a car,' which is the worst thing you can do, because sometimes the most unlikely person is flush...." Gladwell calls it the Warren Harding error, the tendency to make immediate judgments about someone's character or capabilities based on first impressions.

Just as we don't want to prejudge which customers have "client" potential, we don't want to force the issue either. Every relationship builds in its own way and according to its own calendar. Attempts to "greenhouse" a customer into client status could kill the budding flower, rather than grow it. As the song says, "Nice and easy does it, every time." Some will be won over in an instant. Some will take months or even years to grow into a relationship. If someone isn't ready to enter the ranks of our clients, don't push.

There's no reason to push. Clientele development is not the same as database marketing. In fact, it is exactly the opposite. Database marketing relies on compiling as many names as possible in a certain category, with the intention of converting a small percentage of them into customers. Clientele development is the process of handpicking a few people who we deem likely to shop with us on a regular basis, based on our past experience and ongoing relationship,

If contacting the people in our client book feels like an exercise in telemarketing, then we have not correctly identified our clients. Telemarketing is a business built on cold calling strangers and usually presumes a success rate of less than 1 percent. Contacting our clients is about calling people we already know and with whom we've already established some rapport.

"THAT'S COLD CALLING. WALK UP TO THE DOOR. I DON'T EVEN KNOW THEIR NAME. I'M SELLING SOMETHING THEY DON'T EVEN WANT". *Shelly "The Machine" Levine,* **GLENGARRY GLENROSS,** *by David Mamet*

The number of names in our client book is immaterial. Think of many people in the industrial supply business, whose businesses may be built entirely on servicing one or two customers. In truth, a smaller client book is often more effective than a larger one, as it allows us to focus more clearly and use our time more efficiently. The crucial factor is the quality of the customers and the depth of our interactions with them. If we are building relationships and providing real service to the people in our client book, the numbers will grow naturally.

Does all this feel a little exclusive? Maybe even (*gasp!*) elitist? Don't worry. We're not compiling a social Who's Who, or a list of the rich and famous. In fact, it's not even necessary for someone to have made a purchase, to make it to our client list. All we're asking is:

- Do we know the customer and feel comfortable being in contact with them?
- Will the customer recognize us and respond positively to our contact?

If the answer is "yes" to these questions—then we've made a positive identification. It's time to reach out and touch someone.

"*I*" WILL INITIATE
"*Houston, we have Contact...*"

Remember the old days of school dances? Do you recall that awkward, shuffling cluster of boys on one side of the gym and girls on the other—and the invisible dividing line that ran between, transforming the dance floor into an ominous no-go zone? Behold, the human condition on display. Two parties, undeniably interested in one another, yet both unable to make the leap over a barrier that, in fact, exists only in their own minds. Tragedy and comedy intermingled, fear and desire. "Why didn't you call?" versus "I want to be alone."

This is not us. As sellers, we don't have the luxury of playing hard to get. We can't afford to hope that someone else will make the first move. That "someone else" is likely to be the sales associate from across the street, who just invited our client to their store's grand opening. The game has begun and it's our move now. So why is it so hard to make it?

Two reasons, clear and simple. The first is obvious and takes us immediately back to the junior-high dance: fear of rejection. It's undeniable and, unfortunately, inescapable. There is no social interaction without emotional risk, whether it's, "Uh, you wanna, like, um, dance?" or "We're having a reception at the store on Wednesday evening and I do hope we'll see you there." There's always the possibility of an abrupt "no." Or the affront of a dial tone on the other end of the line. Or maybe something even worse…

Actually, it doesn't get any worse. When we confront our ultimate fears, we have to acknowledge that they really don't extend much beyond a slightly impolite refusal or a hang-up. That's about as bad as our rejection can get—which isn't really very bad at all. Ours is not the risk of a lover scorned or a diplomatic overture between nations rebuffed. We're only selling stuff. Even in light of our efforts to make a personal connection with the customer, this is just business.

In fact, a "no" may be as productive as a "yes." A negative response tells us that we either need to work on our approach or on our identification process. Better yet, it tells us immediately that we need to move on and not invest any further time or energy on this particular prospect. Our most dangerous enemy is the response that is vague, polite, and leaves the door half-open and half-closed. In many ways, rejection is our friend. To paraphrase, we have nothing to fear but fear itself.

The second reason we hesitate to reach out to our customers is that we simply aren't sure how. We know we should be in touch. We want to build our business. But we're just not quite clear on how to get the party started. This problem is much easier to solve.

In fact, it's so easy that I'm going to solve it right here in the next few pages. What I'm offering is not a list of suggestions or general concepts. It's a very specific prescription: do this, follow with that, and you'll feel better in the morning. If you're already doing it, then by all means, feel empowered to interpret and adapt the information to your own needs. But if this is your first venture into clientele development, then just do what it says. Without further fanfare, I give you **The Magic Formula: Rapid Response and the 30-60-90 Day Contact Calendar.**

THE *Magic* FORMULA: RAPID RESPONSE *and the* 30-60-90 *Day Contact Calendar*

We've talked about the differences between the direct marketing business and clientele selling, but there is also much we can learn from a business like direct mail. Above all, the direct mail business provides us with a tried-and-true approach to customer contact, built around the inviolable concept of repetition. It's a proven fact: repetition is the key to any customer contact strategy. You can say that again. And again.

Frequent—some might say relentless—customer contact is at the core of the direct marketing business. Just as no company advertises in one magazine one time, no direct marketing company expects to make a sale on their first attempt. The key is familiarity through repetition. It's not about who speaks the loudest or makes the most brash statement. It's who delivers a clear, consistent message, over and over. Go outside and open your mailbox, then beware the deluge. Case closed.

The general rule in most direct marketing circles is that it will take at least three contacts with a customer before a sale is generated. From this, we derive the basis of our magic formula—the Rapid Response, followed by the 30-60-90 Day Contact Calendar.

As the formula makes obvious, the key to our clientele success is consistency. By being in frequent contact, we keep our place in the front, rather than the back, of the customer's mind. This method also reminds us of each client's identity, likes and dislikes, and lifestyle. And it allows us ample opportunity to experiment with a variety of approaches. Three wishes from the genie; third time's the charm— good things seem to come in threes.

This is the best part of the 30-60-90 Day Contact Calendar. It's just so simple. It's hardly so frequent as to have us branded with the scarlet "p." It's sufficient to keep us in the customer's general consciousness. And it's enough time to allow us to assess a customer's real interest. Within three months, a customer will need to make a personal purchase or buy a gift or two. New shipments and styles will arrive in the store. Events or sales will take place. The leaves will grow or fall from the trees. In 30, 60, then 90 days, a client is born.

Step 1. The Rapid Response

When it comes to our first follow-up contact with a customer, sooner is always better. If someone shopped with us today, why would we wait 30 days to contact him or her again? Let's reach out immediately, before yesterday's shopping euphoria fades. After all, it's not hard to know what to say. "Thanks" would be a very good place to start.

The thank-you note is elegant, unassailable, and effective. No one can be offended. No one can be resistant. Given the appalling manners of most of our society, almost everyone will be surprised. It is the perfect means of reinforcing a positive interaction. But it only works if it's done properly—and quickly.

Enter the Rapid Response. I believe that the most effective thank-you note is written and mailed within 48 hours of the transaction. By employing the Rapid Response, we not only send our customer a message of gratitude, but also a whole set of subtle messages about ourselves:

We are special. We are efficient. We are sincere. We are polite. We will be in contact.

"All well and good," the seller responds. "We are also busy." Well, let's hope. Yet, if we are busy, this is all the more reason to write our notes quickly. The longer we postpone, the more likely we are to forget entirely. The more sales go by, the more overwhelmed we will become. The only way to accomplish a consistent timely response is to develop habits. Perhaps the single most effective work habit we can develop is the art of the five-minute thank-you note.

And indeed, it should be a card or a note. While a phone call or e-mail is a perfectly legitimate means of customer contact for our 30-60-90 Day Contact Calendar, the thank-you note is a different animal. Call me Miss Manners, but I believe that a thank-you note benefits from a more formal approach. It should be handwritten and, unlike our other customer contact, should contain no call to action for the customer. It is a simple, sincere expression of personal gratitude.

Dear Mr. Jensen,

It was my pleasure to assist you with your purchase of the locket for your niece. Based upon your description of her, I just know that she'll be delighted. If you have the time, I'd love to hear her reaction. As promised, I will let you know when we receive the matching bracelet, in case you need a gift for her later in the year.

Again, thanks for your purchase. I look forward to having an opportunity to assist you in the future. I am enclosing my business card for your convenience.

Best Regards,

Susan Sullivan

Ladies and gentlemen, set your watches. Now, we're going to copy out the above text by hand on a piece of paper. Go.

Stop. How long did that take? Three minutes? Five? Maybe seven, if we're given to adding our own embellishments. When it comes to customer contact, there is no better investment of energy than a thank-you note. It is time proven, risk proof, and attention getting all at once.

It's also nice. It's worth remembering that any customer who has purchased from us has given us a gift. No matter what we sell, we are not the only person selling it. In almost every case, the customer could have stayed home and made the same purchase from his or her armchair with the push of a few keys on the computer. Effective selling does not involve groveling or offering false flattery to a customer. But a personal expression of gratitude from seller to buyer is not only pleasant; it's appropriate. Someone has done something to our benefit. Let's do like Grandma taught us.

Step 2. The 30-Day Contact

Now it's down to business. It's been four weeks since our last interaction with the customer and it's time to rekindle the flame. Consider the options:

- A **customer care** inquiry—perhaps a phone call to see how the customer is enjoying the purchase, or to make sure Uncle John's gift was well received.
- A **"what's new"** note—maybe a postcard or an e-mail to alert the customer to new merchandise that would be of interest.
- An **invitation**—to a sale, preview, cocktail party, or other store event.

As this is the first attempt at contact, all avenues are available. In most cases, the **customer care** call is the easiest one to make, as it grows directly out of the previous purchase. Like the thank-you note, it establishes us as a considerate, concerned professional. It also gives us a chance to fix anything that's gone wrong, should the customer be less than thrilled with the purchase.

The **"what's new"** note is perhaps the easiest approach to turn directly into a sale, if the new merchandise is a genuine fit for the client. Or, if there is an important event happening in the store, an **invitation** allows us to play host or hostess, and immediately show off the benefits of being one of our valued clients.

The choice is ours. Whatever path we choose, we need to select it in the first 30 days. Then, we need to choose the appropriate route to the customer, which of course should have been gathered as part of the must-have information. If someone has indicated that they prefer to be contacted through the mail or e-mail rather than a telephone call, then do not violate that wish. To do so is to go beyond "pushy" and step into the dreaded red zone: "rude."

Finally, we need to make sure that our contact carries with it an invitation for our client to be in touch. After all, our goal is some kind of response. The only communication that should not contain a call to action is the thank-you note. Any other customer contact must provide some reason for the customer to call us back, or to visit the store, sometime in the next 30 days...

Step 3. The 60-Day Contact

Not to worry. We can't expect our first effort to hit pay dirt. We get three chances, don't we? So if at first we don't succeed, we try again.

But not in the same way. The 30-60-90 Day Contact Calendar gives us three chances to find the path of least resistance for each customer. There's not much point in going down the same road twice. If we led with a customer care inquiry, then this time let's switch to a personal note or invitation. If our 30-day contact was an e-mail about an upcoming sale, then let's try a phone call to let our client know what's new.

Here are a couple of quick notes on the art of "good phone," as they say in Hollywood…

Don't call cold. Prepare.
Determine the objective of the call and the key points to cover *before* you dial the number.

Timing is everything, part 1.
Beware of Sundays, religious holidays, meal times, early hours (before 8:30 a.m.), or late nights (after 9:30 p.m.). *Pay attention to time zones!*

Blessed are the brief.
Identify yourself, ensure that your timing is appropriate, and get to the point quickly. State the reason for the call and why it is relevant to this customer. Then close with a call to action.

Timing is everything, part 2.
If the client is busy, ask when would be a good time to call back. Then do it! Be careful about leaving a message about a gift or sensitive matter. Stick with name, number, and the reason you're calling. Say it with a smile—and a sense of urgency.

When it comes to our 60-day contact, variety is the key. A steady stream of merchandise calls will put us perilously close to "pushy." Too many customer care calls will leave a client wondering if we're aware of a secret defect in the product—a defect that they have yet to uncover. Some clients will want to hear from us only when we have something new to sell them. Some will show up for sales, others for cocktail parties. Some people will respond to e-mails; some prefer phone conversations.

We're searching for a magic formula that gets results and it could take some time to discover. It will not always be the same, even for the same customer. But if we find a method that works, let's make a note of it in our client books. If we don't, then it's back to the lab...

Step 4. The 90-Day Contact

If we haven't seen the customer in 90 days, and haven't had a response to our customer care call or our merchandise suggestion, now would be the moment to put subtlety aside. Our client is MIA. It's time to send out the search party.

Our 90-day contact is a direct appeal for our long-lost friend to phone home. We need to be as straightforward as possible, expressing our desire to reconnect. This is essentially a customer care call. Our script is simple:

> *We miss you.*
> *Let's get in touch.*

Remember, the goal of our 30-60-90 Day Contact Calendar is to receive a response. We don't have to make a sale (not that there's anything wrong with that). The important thing is that our client indicates a desire to be a part of this relationship. It could be as simple as a return call to say, "Would love to stop by the sale but am out of town right now." Fine. But we need to hear something. It takes two to tango. We want to be sure that our partner is at least hearing the music.

The true value of this monthly regimen is that it places us in a proactive, informed position to determine who really belongs in our client book. We are not at the mercy of luck, accident, or wishful thinking. If we don't have contact after 90 days and three attempts, it's safe to assume that our client is lost in space. Meanwhile, back in the real world, we can turn our attention to better things—now a little bit wiser and even more determined to cultivate that next name in our book.

Friends, like promises, should be kept.

"*I*" WILL INDIVIDUALIZE
"*Let's Get Personal.*"

If all this sounds a little too simple…it is. As most of us learned back in the days of school dances, it's not just about identifying our prospect and taking some initiative. The art is in the approach. What will differentiate us from the hundreds of direct marketers using the same 30-60-90 Day Contact Calendar? What will allow us to command our client's attention amidst the clutter of catalogs, commercials, and corporate come-ons? Believe it or not, we have the secret weapon already in our possession—and it's stronger than the mightiest mailing list:

The personal touch.

The bigger things get, the better it is to be small. Sometimes amidst all the shouting, it's the whisper that gets heard. We are so accustomed to being the targets of marketing and advertising campaigns that we have built up our own resistance. In an instant, we pick out the fake "personalized" letter or the telemarketer reading from his prompter and tune out just as quickly. (During the last election, it was not actually the mayor leaving us a phone message. We were not fooled.)

There is only one way to build a clientele, and that is personally—one individual at a time. In a mailbox full of solicitations, a handwritten thank-you note will be read. On an answering machine overloaded with invitations, a personal message about something specifically of interest to the listener will earn a response. In a world of one size fits all, we're offering bespoke service, and this is what will set us apart. The more "mass" marketing becomes, the more power is wielded by the lone individual with a pen and a personal approach.

Certainly, any interaction we have with our client must be professional. It must conform to the image our company wants to present. But from our rapid-response thank-you note, to our 90-day "we miss you call," and hopefully beyond, every interaction with our client should be individualized and delivered with a personal touch.

Our notes and calls should be simple and friendly, and contain three key elements. Here's an example of a 30-day "what's new" note. If you like the form, feel free to copy it and then customize it to each customer. But first, see if you can identify the three elements:

> Dear Mrs. Snodgrass:
>
> I was thinking of you this week and thought I would drop you a note to say hello. I haven't seen you in a while, and I wanted to let you know that we have received our fall collection of cashmere sweaters. There is one in the exact shade of lime green that you like so well! I know you will love it.
>
> At your convenience, please stop by the store, as it would be very nice to see you again.
>
> Best Regards,
>
> Tom Atkins

Admittedly, Mrs. Snodgrass is not likely to frame this and hang it on her wall. But it will work, because it contains the three key elements that should be a part of any communication that we have with our customer, whether it's written or verbal:

- It has a personal touch.
- It has a reminder.
- It has a WIFM.

Of course, the personal touch extends though every element of the correspondence. It is handwritten and the envelope is hand-addressed, which is why someone will open it and not toss it in the pile of credit offers and notifications of sweepstakes winnings. It is personalized to the customer—using his or her preferred name and correct spelling. Most importantly…

It reminds the customer of his or her shopping experience with us. Whether it's a recollection from the conversation, an answer to a question the customer had, or a reference to an important event in the customer's life, we need something to stir the customer's memory of our interaction. This is why we always keep our "I" on the client when we're on the selling floor. Throughout the transaction, we should be thinking ahead to our follow-up, knowing that we'll need a few pieces of personal information to include in our note.

If we were to just leave things there, we would have done something polite and professional but not terribly productive. If our correspondence is to go beyond a social grace to a selling strategy, it needs something more. We need a WIFM.

EVEWYBODY WUVS a "WIFM".

Translation: "What's In it For Me?" No, not for us. For the customer. Every communication with the customer should include a WIFM: a reason why it's in the client's interests to do what we're inviting them to do. We have to offer an incentive to encourage the customer to continue the relationship and come back to shop again soon. Again, this must be personalized for each individual customer. The WIFM should directly engage the interests or needs of this particular customer. It could be notification of a new product, an upcoming sale, a gift idea, or a store event. Anything that will demonstrate to the customer the value of this client/seller relationship is a valid WIFM.

But first, let's check ourselves. Remember, a WIFM does not mean what's in it for us. This is *not about us*. It's all about the customer. Things that are *not* WIFMs:

> **"New merchandise has arrived."** This is of interest to *us*. It is not inherently of interest to our client. Now, if that new merchandise includes something that would be fitting for our customer, then we've found a WIFM.

> **"Just one more good sale, and we'll hit our numbers."** End-of-the-month calls with vaguely worded messages about "great new things to show you" are every bit as transparent as they seem. Our "I's" are crossed and staring directly at ourselves.

"There's an incentive to whoever sells this overstocked item." Our client does not exist to help us win the new set of steak knives. We need to find a specific reason that this item would be useful for this particular client.

The WIFM is the ultimate example of Taking the "I" Out of Clientele. Properly used, it is where everything we've discussed comes together to move us from transactional selling to relationship selling. We won't even try to select the right WIFM until we learn to take our own needs out of the process, and begin to see the customer's interests rather than our own. We can't find the WIFM until we have sufficient information about our client and his or her lifestyle.

Once we're ready to put our "I" into action, no customer communication will be complete without something in it for the client. The personal touch is a little good form, a hint of flattery, and always a bit of substance. The substance is the WIFM, and it's what will keep 'em coming back for more.

"*I*" WILL INCREASE
There's More where that came from...

And more. And more. Don't quit while you're ahead. When it comes to making sales, it is indeed the more the merrier, and our goal should always be to maximize the customer's shopping experience and our own relationship-building efforts. The key to increasing sales is not to find more clients. If we're following the Don'ts and Do's of Selling, this will take care of itself. The key to increasing sales is to get more out of each client that we have.

Always Be CLOSING? *No.* ALWAYS BE *Enhancing!*

It's all a matter of changing our mindset. Remember, the game is not over when the cash register rings. Once a customer has made a purchase, we know that what we're doing is working. We have built a rapport, determined needs, and provided solutions. We have gathered information and learned about likes and dislikes, and we are about to make at least an initial entry on our client's inventory of purchases. The table is set and the guests have arrived in good spirits—but the party has not yet begun. Now, it's time to make a good thing better.

Like putting makeup on a supermodel, it's always easier to enhance than to create something from scratch. Once we've made a sale, we've done most of the heavy lifting already. Now that the customer has something in his or her hand, it's not hard to think of what might complement it. Let's start with the obvious: shirts beget ties, shoes beget bags, china begets silver, computers beget service contracts. Smart companies create products that need other products. It all goes together—people needing people, people needing products, products needing other products.

But there's more to it than that. What we've just described are add-ons and they're hardly a new concept in selling. That's why those little baskets of small, inexpensive items are sitting right next to the cash-wrap. Ultimately, we're aiming at something a little bit deeper. We're trying to enhance the sale. That doesn't just mean making it bigger. It means making it better, more meaningful, or more satisfying. Add-ons tend to be about us. Enhancements are about the customer.

This is where our **intelligence** and **information** turn into **action**. The goal is not simply to find another item to match up with the one we've sold. The goal is to find another item that meets a need or interest of the customer. What have we learned about our client in the course of our interaction? Favorite colors? Travel plans? Hobbies? Is Mrs. Kowalsky's son getting married? Perhaps she needs an engagement gift. Has the Jerry Maguire wannabe seen our new high-tech pen? What better corporate gift for his clients, when they ink their multimillion dollar contract? Don't get me started. I could enhance all night.

The value of enhancing is multifold. It shows our customer that we've been listening. It elevates what could have been a simple transaction into an experience. And it establishes us as an ally, demonstrating our understanding of what our client is after and our ability to help realize that desire. Because it relates directly to a client's interests, enhancing will always protect us from plunging into "pushy." Add-ons are "pushy." Enhancements are just that—an extra added bit of positive relationship building. No one complains about the cherry on top of the whipped cream.

We are not asking the question, "Is there anything else I can show you?" By now, we should know what our customer needs to see. Instead, let's make an invitation or a suggestion, like:

> *"You mentioned that your sheets needed to be replaced. Let me show you a pattern that looks fabulous with that duvet cover."*

"You really should see the new candles we just got in. They'd be the perfect hostess gift tonight."

Enhancing is a matter of passion. It should fuel our client's interest in our product and demonstrate our own enthusiasm for the relationship and the merchandise. Any product we show to enhance a sale should be something for which we believe the customer will have a passion, or something for which we ourselves have a passion. So let's invite our client to see it, not ask for permission to show it.

Taking the "I" Out of Clientele is a process of planting seeds. To make one sale but miss the enhancement is like growing the tree but forgetting to pick the fruit. Anyone can clerk a sale. Only those who've invested the effort in learning who the customer is and what they're after can enhance a sale.

To start, we must **identify** our clients, because life is too short and the world too big to pursue everyone. We have to focus our efforts on people who know us, and who have purchased from us or expressed an interest in purchasing in the future. To nurture the client relationship, we **initiate** contact, through a Rapid Response thank-you note for the first purchase, followed by use of the 30-60-90 Day Contact Calendar. We get results because we **individualize** our communication. No mass mailings or cold-calls for us. We use our intelligence to offer a WIFM that is custom-fit for each client.

Finally, we **increase** our sales by enhancing each transaction with an invitation. Using all our knowledge of the customer and the trust that we've established in the relationship, we go beyond providing the customer with the product they need—we show them something they'll love. Don't waste all the work we've done by walking away too soon. Every good story needs a clever twist at the end. So does every good sales transaction.

Conclusion

Have we somehow ended up too far from where we started? After all, we began by talking about building relationships and turning customers into friends, and wound up discussing strategies to expand the sale. Somewhere along the way, did we let our "I" wander away from the customer and turn right back to ourselves?

Not at all. But let's admit that keeping ourselves out of the picture is easier said than done. Putting ourselves front and center comes naturally and it's a hard habit to break. The only way we can get ourselves off center stage is through utilizing specific actions and strategies that force us to change our style of selling.

It's a little like a diet. Most of us would not struggle to identify what might have brought on those extra pounds (more cake, anyone?) or what general changes in our daily routine might help reverse our unwanted personal expansion program. Those are usually obvious. The real challenge is in changing our behavior. Even with the best of intentions, temptation will come to call. Exceptions will be made. Soon we'll find ourselves reverting to our old, familiar ways.

> **"THAT'S WHAT I'M SAYIN'. THE *old* WAYS. THE *old* WAYS... *sell* HIM... *sell* HIM... MAKE HIM SIGN THE CHECK."** *Shelly "The Machine" Levine,* **GLENGARRY GLENROSS,** *by David Mamet*

When it comes to losing weight, we don't need general knowledge about nutrition. We need a diet—a specific course of action, a regimen to follow, and probably a weekly "weigh-in" to keep us honest. It may be uncomfortable. At times we will complain. But if we stick with it, we will begin to develop new, healthier habits to replace our old ones. First it will be a matter of discipline and effort. Then gradually the habits will become part of our lifestyle. We will have a new way of eating.

Ah, that's it! Taking the "I" Out of Clientele begins as a philosophy, becomes a course of action, and finally, turns into our manner of selling. It's not possible to instantly change our mindset. We start by changing our daily routine. If we like the results we see, our new habits will be reinforced. Before we know it, we will have changed our point of view. Here is one more "I" word with which to conclude: *integration*.

Integration

The Don'ts and Do's of Selling, the information-gathering, the clientele book, the 30-60-90 Day Contact Calendar, the enhancement of the sale—all of these things are means to an end. They are strategies and techniques that will continually remind us to refocus our efforts on developing the client relationship.

Initially, some of our actions will feel forced or contrived. They will make us self-conscious, in the best of ways—we will be aware of what we're doing throughout the selling process. But as we persist and as we review our results, we will find ourselves integrating them into our own personal style and, more importantly, adapting our own personal style to a more client-centered approach.

I recently counseled a sales associate who, after some initial resistance, was beginning to embrace a more relationship-oriented selling style. Still, she was frustrated at some of the setbacks. She was working hard to determine the customer's needs but struggling to enhance the sale. Upon a later review of one particular transaction, she identified several items that might have been of interest to the customer—but she had failed to gather the must-have contact information in order to follow up.

She viewed that interaction as a failure. I viewed it as a breakthrough. "Margie, look at the change in your thinking! Three weeks ago, you weren't even trying to determine needs or enhance the sale. You certainly weren't reviewing your transactions to see what you could have improved. It wouldn't have occurred to you to contact the customer about an item of interest."

I concluded with a pep talk. "Obviously, you want to improve. Now that you've seen the importance of the contact information, you'll be sure to get it next time. The important thing is that you've changed your point of view. Your focus is on the client and you're seeing how all of the selling skills fit together. This is progress!"

So let's end right back where we began, with the realization that in matters of selling, and life in general, it's not all about us. And let's add a little proviso: it does indeed *start* with us. It will be our action that kindles the spark of the relationship, our efforts that fan the flames, and our interest that keeps the fire burning. If we make the invitation, our customers will respond.

More importantly, if we make the invitation, we will respond. Our attitude will change to follow our action. Subconsciously, we will begin to see the selling process, and maybe life in general, as an event at which we are the host, not the guest. We are in control but we also are responsible for the comfort and care of others. We are not waiting for someone else to make introductions and pass the *hors d'oeuvres*. Taking the "I" Out of Clientele is a process of integrating intelligence and action to serve not our own interests, but those of our client.

As a retail lifer, one of my favorite movies is the holiday classic, *Miracle on 34th Street*. Remember when Kris Kringle, the Santa Claus at Macy's, begins sending customers to other stores, all in the selfless spirit of Christmas? Do you remember what happens next? Suddenly, Macy's business is booming, awash in goodwill and newly devoted customers.

Whether it's in the movies or real life, nothing stands out more than generosity and nothing gets better results. Putting our focus on the client will always be worth the effort. Whether it's making sales or making friends, the payoff is the same. After all, the relationship is the reward.

Cheryl Beall is the founder of Retail 101, a consulting company offering common sense solutions to specialty retailers. With over 15 years of experience as a senior retail executive with Bergdorf Goodman, Hermes, Montblanc, and Loro Piana, Cheryl has developed sales and clientele programs for many of the world's most prestigious luxury brands. She is a resident of New York City.

978-0-595-41369-0
0-595-41369-2